The name says it all! "Soul Food Sessions". Niya sets the table for women to release, relax, rejuvenate, and to be revived. Far too many women are guilty of nourishing others while they go empty. The retreat featured deliciously crafted "Soul Food" Sessions specifically designed to replenish the total woman. Every session had its own unique component, but they all worked in harmony with each other. Soul Food Sessions Retreat is all about re-establishing healthy connections with your mind, body, and spirit. I witnessed transformation. I witnessed healing from rejection and abandonment. I witnessed women from various walks of life all feasting on what they needed most and that's SOUL FOOD!

— *Evangelist Latrice Ryan*

It is imperative for women to support each other, not only in deed, but in testimony. Niya's Soul Food Sessions is a space where women can share their stories, not just to free themselves, but to testify to show others they too can be free. This is why I would recommend women all around the country to attend Niya's Soulfood Sessions.

— *Founder of Impact*
Tunisha Brown

Seasoned with Grace Edition...

Soulfood
Sessions

21 DAY DEVOTIONAL TO ELEVATE YOUR LIFE

NIYA BROWN MATTHEWS

WWW.13THANDJOAN.COM

Soulfood Sessions. Niya Brown Matthews.

13th & Joan books may be purchased for educational, business or sales promotional use. For information, please email the Sales Department at sales@13thandjoan.com.

Printed in the U.S. A.
First Printing, June 2018

Library of Congress Cataloging-in-Publication Data has been applied for.
ISBN

Dedication

To all the women who attended my Soulfood
Sessions with Niya Retreats and Brunches.
Thank you for entrusting me to help you
restore what was lost, empower the BOSS
within, and to inspire you to become better
versions of yourselves.

Acknowledgements

I am grateful for God giving me the vision to write this book. God speaks to me in a way I can interpret for my readers to understand. This book was done in obedience to God's word. To my dear husband Eric, my daughter Jazlyn and friend Tara for believing in my vision and pushing me to keep going. I knew our numerous conversations, brainstorming, and prayers would all pay off to complete this first of many series of self help books.

Introduction

I wrote this book to help guide you into your greatness with a sprinkle of grace. Life can be so hard at times, and we far too often find ourselves overwhelmed. In this space, we neglect the very thing that's tearing us down... we neglect OURSELVES. I wanted to give you some empowering nuggets and inspirational vitamins to help you cope and and look at life through a different lens.

In my walk I've seen people "mask" or "filter" their issues, and through avoidance bigger giants are created. Before you know it, you feel defeated by those giants. Reading this book will remind you that God has not forgotten about them and through his GRACE we can and will overcome. This book is for anyone seeking inspiration to become better, mind, body and soul.

God's grace is always sufficient, despite how big the obstacle may seem. We all have moments when we are weak.

Sometimes we feel like we can't do anything right. No matter what the enemy says, we are not slaves to him. His Grace will always keep us out of bondage.

While writing this book, I have pondered many things. Much of what the ladies who attend my Soulfood Sessions Retreat and Brunches, disclose that they are facing. Why are so many women/men broken or going through so much turmoil? I was reminded of 2 Timothy: 3, when Paul was writing the 21 sins that shows the exceeding wickedness of self sin. I want you to read a chapter a day for 21 days, to help you become better, wiser. Doing this, can help you to fight against allowing that very "thing" to hold you back from being a better version of you. Doing this can remind you how important it is to love yourself.

I see so many people under pressure to be what others want them to be. Whether through society, employers, family members, friends, and even our children, we are pulled in many different directions. Our tanks are running on empty and everyone is looking for someone to help empower and encourage them to keep pressing forward. There are people in search of validation from others because they lack self-love. This book will help elevate your mind and give you a positive outlook on life.

10

Alpha

You can't thrive if you are always pouring out. It's now time to receive some encouraging words that elevate your life.

12

21 Day
Devotional

Get your tools
ready, God is
going to send you
the work.

Day
one

REFLECTIVE THOUGHT OF THE DAY:

You can't use prayer to replace laziness.

Soulfood:

If you really want to be successful in anything you need to be ready for it. Success is the result of hard work, learning from failure, loyalty, and persistence. The scripture comes to mind:

"Faith without works is dead"
(James 2:14-26).

Don't ask God to shift the atmosphere if you're not willing to move your feet. Greatness is available to you, but you have to be open to receive it.

Affirmation:
Nothing worth having comes easy.
If I put in the time and effort, I will
see the results.

Use the lines below to create a list of what goals you want to complete. Now let's speak LIFE over these goals. Remember who you are and that God lives within you. Stop running scared. Start walking in your authority. Each time you complete a goal listed, remember to celebrate along the way! YOU DID THAT!

_____

_____

_____

_____

_____

_____

_____

_____

_____

_____

_____

_____

_____

You are here to do something you are uniquely created for. No one else can do it like you can. That's why you are here.

Day
two

REFLECTIVE THOUGHT OF THE DAY:
Stop comparing yourself to people with a different track, different destination, and different hurdles. If you are following your God given purpose, then there is no competition. Your lane is yours, and their lane is theirs.

Soulfood:
♡

We all have a dynamic purpose over our lives. No one was created the same. We are uniquely different. Often time's people compare their success with others and find themselves either competing or feeling let down because they haven't accomplished what others have. You may even think everyone is better than you, not realizing what you are seeing is the image they portray to others. Everyone has their own fears and weaknesses.

Affirmation:
True happiness is found when you stop comparing yourself to other people. True beauty begins the moment you decide to be yourself.

Imagine that your 100 year old self had access to a time machine. They jumped into that time machine and arrived to this very moment in time. They climb out, sit next to you, and give you advice. What would they say? Write it down.

Now take that advice and create a list of action. What you will see emerge is, in essence, what gives your life some sense of meaning. Now begin living and moving towards a more fulfilling, purpose-lead life.

_____

_____

_____

_____

_____

_____

_____

_____

_____

_____

_____

_____

Show me your friends, and I'll show you your future.
—Mark Ambrose

Day
three

REFLECTIVE THOUGHT OF THE DAY:
Get around people who add to your life.
Be intentional about filling yourself up
and choose your friends wisely. This
scripture comes to mind:
"He who walks with wise men will be wise,
but the companion of fools will suffer
harm" (Proverbs 13:20).

23

Soulfood: ♡

Stay away from negative people. They have a problem for every solution.

Affirmation:

Today I choose to associate myself with people who inspire me and challenge me to rise higher and make me better. I am no one's door mat. I deserve more.

Write down the 5 people you spend the most time with. Do those 5 people make me a better person? If not, start today by walking with the dreamers, the believers, the courageous, the cheerful, the planners, the doers, and the successful people. Change your circle, change your life.

_____

_____

_____

_____

_____

_____

_____

_____

_____

_____

_____

_____

_____

_____

The words you speak become the house you live in.

—Hafiz

Day
four

REFLECTIVE THOUGHT OF THE DAY:

The Power of life and death is in the tongue. Spend less time speaking complaints and more time speaking solutions. I am sure you heard this scripture:

"Death and life are in the power of the tongue, and those who love it will eat its fruit" (Proverbs 18:21). If you spend a lot of time complaining, you'll find yourself worse off than you initially started and having no energy at all. It pulls so much out of you. I've seen people even go to the extent of posting their issues on social media where it grows legs and people want to add their 2 cents which just intensifies it. The best solution is to go directly to the source of the problem. Often times the reason for the complaints is issues like being afraid, overwhelmed, and or rejection.

Soulfood: ♡

The words that come out of our mouth go
into our own ears as well as other people's,
and then they drop down into our soul
where they give us either joy or sadness,
peace or upset, depending on the types of
words we have spoken.

Affirmation:
*Today let's speak LIFE
into the atmosphere.*

1. Instead of complaining, try venting.
Get it out so you're not stuck with it.

2. Choose thoughts and words
that will lead to a solution.

3. Instead of complaining, you can choose to
remember all of the blessings that you have.

_____

_____

_____

_____

_____

_____

_____

_____

_____

_____

_____

_____

_____

_____

What you tell
yourself everyday
will either lift you
up or tear
you down.

Day
five

REFLECTIVE THOUGHT OF THE DAY:
Be careful who you
have speaking
into your life. They can
help or harm your process.

Soulfood:
♡

Words influence others and build relationships. They can tear down relationships if not used wisely; they have the power to manifest change, whether it's good or bad. Be mindful of who you let into your ear gates. You have "sly slick" folks and "hating" folks who may not want you to do better than them, so they will fill your ear gates with negativity to hinder you from excelling. Don't allow their jealous tendencies to stop you from walking in your purpose, your destiny.

Affirmation:

Today I choose to protect my ear gates. I will also resist from speaking ill will of others and gossiping. I will choose words that build up, not tear down. I declare I will offer myself the same empathy and compassion I'd extend to anyone else.

If you have some negative Nancys in your circle of friends, limit the time you spend with them or find better friends. Negative energy has a way of dragging everything surrounding it in, like a big black hole. Avoid it when you can. Surround yourself with positive uplifting people.

_____

_____

_____

_____

_____

_____

_____

_____

_____

_____

_____

_____

_____

_____

Your hardest times often lead to the greatest moments in your life. Keep going. Tough situations build strong people in the end.

Day

six

REFLECTIVE THOUGHT OF THE DAY:

They have moved on. Life has gone. Staying stuck in anger is punishing you. Release so you can live. Past anger—whether a grudge, resentment, or pent-up rage—or a slight committed by someone you were close to years ago and never forgave is like having a book bag full of bricks hanging on your back. The people and situations you haven't moved past can create emotional and physical problems that will affect your health and lead you to act that anger out on innocent people who love and support you.

Soulfood:

Let go of blame or resentment, and you'll feel as though several boulders have been lifted from your shoulders.

Affirmation:
Today I choose to Let Go, Forgive, and RELEASE! It no longer has a place in my life!

1. Write down your emotions and what's going on in the inside without judging them.

2. Share with someone you trust. Get it off your chest.

3. Find your new truth, giving yourself a chance to set things right within.

4. Have a release ceremony. At one of my Soul-food Sessions events in Atlanta, I passed a brick around to the Attendees and that brick represented the weight that was binding them. They had to call it out by its name—that was their way of releasing it in the atmosphere. You can be creative and pick an activity that works for you. For example, throw rocks in a safe place somewhere, or find a private space to shake your limbs to release the negative thing that's holding you back from moving on and living your life to the fullest.

_____
_____
_____
_____
_____
_____
_____

Not my will,
but thine will
be done.

Day
seven

REFLECTIVE THOUGHT OF THE DAY:

Stop praying for things
and people than can never
fulfill you. It's time to RESET
your prayer life. Mature in
the Spirit.

Soulfood:

People are quick to give up on praying when they don't see immediate answers. Maybe God is answering your prayers; He's simply saying no. Or maybe He's saying it's not the right time. Or maybe He's saying, "I'm not going to remove that obstacle until you change your attitude and quit complaining about it." Stay Faithful. Make some adjustments, and you will see things begin to improve in HIS time. I've seen people jump into relationships or a business deal that they didn't feel good about, but they wanted it so badly. God is a gentleman. If you insist, He will back off and let you do things your way. Most of the time when we do that, we end up settling for second best. Trust your gut. This scripture comes to mind:

"For this reason, since the day we heard about you, we have not stopped praying for you and asking God to fill you with the knowledge of His will in all spiritual wisdom and understanding, so that you may walk in a manner worthy of the Lord and may please Him in every way: bearing fruit in every good work, growing in the knowledge of God"
(Colossians 1:9-10).

Affirmation:

Lord, remove anybody out of my life that means me ill will, serves me no purpose, and is not real or loyal. Bless me with the discernment to realize and give me the strength to let go and don't look back.

Don't stop praying. Praying is a powerful thing. Ask God for the spiritual wisdom before you make a decision about anything. Make prayer a lifestyle.

_____
_____
_____
_____
_____
_____
_____
_____
_____
_____
_____
_____

A bad attitude can literally block love, blessings, and destiny from finding you. Don't be the reason you don't succeed.

—Mandy Hale

Day
eight

REFLECTIVE THOUGHT OF THE DAY:
A bad attitude can block you
from some good opportunities.
Settle your spirit and stop
sabotaging yourself.

Soulfood:

You can be a beautiful person on the outside, but if you have a bad attitude, no one will find you attractive. Attitudes affect the atmosphere and mood around you. If you carry a vibe that suggests that you lack confidence, others will pick that up. What you think about yourself determines your attitude.

Affirmation:

Today I am deciding to change the way I view myself. I am intelligent, valuable, likable, built for success, important, strong, and resilient.

Write down the things that give you an "attitude." Now every day before you interact with anyone, make a conscience effort to find something positive about that thing. Your brain controls your mind. What you put into your brain on a constant basis will either produce negative energy or positive energy. Talk to yourself and speak the right things over your life.

_____

_____

_____

_____

_____

_____

_____

_____

_____

_____

_____

_____

_____

Do not bring people into your life who weighs you down. And trust your instincts. Good relationships feel good. They feel right. They don't hurt.

—Michelle Obama

Day
nine

REFLECTIVE THOUGHT OF THE DAY:

There is no better feeling than eliminating all the dead weight in your life. I am referring to toxic and negative relationships that bring hardly any value or significance to your life. All of the negative and time-consuming habits that play virtually no role in helping you get to where you want to go. You've wasted enough days on these toxic people. It's time to RELEASE!

Soulfood:

You will be elevated as soon as you stop clinging to the place where you are not appreciated. Knowing your worth will allow you to make better choices.

Affirmation:
I will get to where I'm going if that means dropping you. I love you, but I love me more.

Write down a big letter Y on one side and an N on the other side. Begin to think of everyone that you talk to often whether on the phone or in person and ask yourself if they help you get to where you want to go or hold you back. If they added value to your life, write their name down under the Y category. If they were negative and seemed to always have something discouraging to say, they would go underneath the N category. Y stood for yes and N stood for no. If your N category is getting longer than what you had for the Y category, it means you have an enormous amount of dead weight in your personal relationships that is drastically holding you back from moving forward to achieve the success that you deeply desire.

_____

_____

_____

_____

_____

_____

_____

_____

Trust where God is leading you and that this year will be a great one.

Day
ten

REFLECTIVE THOUGHT OF THE DAY:
Lean not on your own
understanding and trust
the process.

Soulfood:

We live in a world where trust must be earned and seems to be in short supply. But Solomon, the famous king who wrote Proverbs, knew that trust is exactly where we must start. This scripture come to mind:

> *"Trust in the LORD with all your heart and do not lean on your own understanding"* (Proverbs 3:5).

Have you ever tried your way and made a mess of it? Thinking, if you had just waited, a lot of what we went through could have been avoided? I believe we all have been through this in one shape or form. Most of us have faced disappointments, which have taught us that we can only depend upon ourselves. But living the life God has called us to means unlearning that lesson. Instead, we're meant to rest in God's understanding. to be open to receive it.

Affirmation:
Acknowledge Him in all the ways possible, and he shall direct destiny's paths.

Surrender yourself and all your troubles. Let Him be the Master of you and of everything in your life. Once you stop trying to do things in your own strength, God will take over and lift you to new heights. Replace negative thoughts with positive ones. Ask God to give you patience.

_____

_____

_____

_____

_____

_____

_____

_____

_____

_____

We carry our own bags and choose to walk together.

Day
eleven

REFLECTIVE THOUGHT OF THE DAY:
Stop trying to carry everyone. No heavy lifting should be displayed! You'll ruin your back on people who need to learn to walk. Pray for their strength to do it own their own.

Soulfood:

♡

We cannot fix others and sometimes, despite our good intentions, we can cause more harm than good if we enable or control. Allow room for people to grow. You can always encourage and help someone up but understand they have to want to move first.

Affirmation:
Help me help you!

Write down a list of people you are constantly helping (it may even be your kindred). Now ask yourself if you are tired of carrying someone else's "bags." You may realize it is time to set some responsibilities or worries down. It is time for you to extend love but set healthy boundaries with others so they learn to pick up their own bags. Walk with them, not for them. I know it sounds easier said than done. Walking away or distancing yourself from people who are having a negative impact on your life can be a difficult thing to do, but it can also prove to be extremely empowering and rewarding in the long run. Give it a try.

_____

_____

_____

_____

_____

_____

_____

_____

_____

_____

_____

_____

Let us occupy ourselves entirely in knowing God. The more we know him, the more we will desire to know him. As love increases with knowledge, the more we know God, the more we will truly love him. We will learn to love him equally in times of distress or in times of great joy.

—Brother Lawrence

Day
twelve

REFLECTIVE THOUGHT OF THE DAY:
Prayer is like planting a seed.
Don't dig it up to see how it is
doing. Pray for it. Release it by
giving thanks.

Soulfood:

Prayer can be hard for some. I remember not knowing what to say when I was praying. I would go to bible study with my grandmother and watch how she would just moan or sing until the Holy Spirit showed up. Whether it's those mumbled words, a moan or a song, our prayer lives reveal so much about our relationship with God. But we get busy in the hustle and bustle with daily life. Often prayer gets lost in the jumble of life—we get busy, lazy, or distracted. But with all that's going on in this world, it's time to activate or re-activate that prayer life.

Affirmation:

Today I declare I am not going to give up praying even when it feels as if I have not received an answer in a timely manner. But I must persevere in asking for God's help, even if it seems He is delaying His response, for the Lord may just be waiting to see persistent prayer before He acts.

Choose a specific place to pray away from distractions so you can concentrate. Be specific, persistent, and consistent in your daily prayers incorporating these tips:

1. Know to whom you are speaking.

2. Thank him.

3. Ask for God's will.

4. Say what you need.

5. Ask for forgiveness.

6. Pray with a friend.

7. Pray the Word.

8. Memorize Scripture.

_____

_____

_____

_____

_____

_____

_____

_____

_____

_____

_____

Make more
moves and fewer
announcements.

Day
thirteen

REFLECTIVE THOUGHT OF THE DAY:

Stop announcing your every move. If you want to protect it, be private with it.

Soulfood:

♡

Do you know people can pray for your downfall? The "sly slick" haters can't stand to see you shine. Be very careful with announcing your every move. There are people who will try to sabotage you just because of their "hating" spirit. It may seem unnatural to keep your intentions and plans private, but try it. If you do tell a friend, make sure not to say it as a satisfaction.

Affirmation:

Learn to develop tunnel vision and focus on the mission. Use your creative energy to come up with new and more effective ways to get the job done. Be innovative.

Here are a few practical tips on how to remain focused while pursuing your dream:

1. Find a quiet place to meditate and pray

2. Keep an organized space

3. Make a to do list

4. Prioritize your tasks

5. Manage your time

6. Make time for breaks

7. Don't procrastinate

8. Stop allowing your personal space to be a dumping ground for other people's drama

9. Multitask less so you can increase productivity

10. Eat and drink plenty of water—take breaks

_____

_____

_____

_____

A leader is one
who knows the
way, goes the way,
and shows the way.
—John C Maxwell

Day
fourteen

REFLECTIVE THOUGHT OF THE DAY:

Are you a true "Boss" or Leader?" Do you possess the true traits to give yourself that title? True leader's desire is to achieve above and beyond expectations. If you're a REAL "BOSS," you need to be self-motivated, and no one else can do that for you except yourself. One of my favorite quotes is from Maya Angelou:

"Nothing will work unless you do."

Soulfood:

Integrity, high standards, confidence, optimism, positivity, accountability, courage, respectable, passion, are some traits that make up one amazing leader. However, a true leader inspires greatness in others. They are not worried about someone taking their "shine." I used to tell my staff I'm only as strong as my team. I believe in helping others tap into their full potential and we ALL WIN! Or a better one:

*"Team work makes the
dream work!"*

Affirmation:
*Helping others won't dull my shine.
What's for me is for me, and what's
for you is for you.*

Do some random acts of kindness.

Help a stranger.

Provide a resource for someone looking to improve their life.

Give a stranger a compliment.

Sow a seed in your community.

Mentor a child or teen.

_____

_____

_____

_____

_____

_____

_____

_____

_____

_____

_____

_____

No one is you

and that is

your power.

Day
fifteen

REFLECTIVE THOUGHT OF THE DAY:
What others think about you is not important. What you think about yourself means everything.

Soulfood:

Deep inside of us, along with our need to be liked, we also have a need to be authentic, to think and live in our own unique way. Being true to your whole self isn't easy. It takes courage and perseverance, but in the long run, it feels better. And for many people, bringing their unique offerings to the world is what gives their life meaning. God divinely created you to be You uniquely. When we start to rely on what other people think of us, and we make their opinion pivotal to our success, we get into trouble. We start tailoring our lives to fit the expectations. That's when issues arise.

Accept your uniqueness. It's ok to be different. No one is better at being you than YOU!

Take a moment to think and write down your attributes, things you love about yourself. Now every day look in the mirror and say that "thing" out loud. Start doing this EVERYDAY! Now start believing it.

_____
_____
_____
_____
_____
_____
_____
_____
_____
_____
_____
_____
_____

Strength and growth only comes through continuous effort and struggle.

Day
sixteen

REFLECTIVE THOUGHT OF THE DAY:

"Where there is no struggle, there is no strength" is one of my favorite quotes from Oprah Winfrey. She was a woman who was told she was "unfit" for television by her boss and fired her. Most would have given up, but she PUSHED through it. Be inspired by her. Push through what tries to stop you.

Soulfood:

Every struggle in your past has shaped you into the person you are today. Take God's hand and step into your future without fear. Stop worrying and doubting. Have faith that things will work out. Maybe not how you planned, but the way it's meant to be. I want to encourage you to not give up. Victory comes to those who endure the journey from vision to manifestation.

Affirmation:

My past doesn't dictate my future the same way other's opinion don't dictate your future. As a child of God, you have something most people don't have: a connection to the one that can transform situations and make them work out for my good. The Bible says, " And we know that God causes everything to work together for those who love God and are called to his purpose for them" (Romans 8:28). If you put your faith and confidence in God, you have the right to feel confident and excited about your future.

Beauty comes in all different types. There are many ways to be beautiful, both on the inside and on the outside. When something about you is appealing to others, whether it's your looks, or your witt, or your personality, or your kindness, that's a beautiful thing. List some ways that you are beautiful, either on the inside or the outside.

_____
_____
_____
_____
_____
_____
_____
_____
_____
_____
_____
_____
_____
_____
_____
_____

You are only confined by the walls you build yourself.

Day

seventeen

REFLECTIVE THOUGHT OF THE DAY:
The sooner you step away from you comfort zone you'll realize that it really wasn't all that comfortable.

Soulfood:

The ability to take risks by stepping outside your comfort zone is the primary way by which we grow. But we are often afraid to take that first step. In truth, comfort zones are not really about comfort: they are about fear. We all struggle with fear of something. For me it was the fear of success. I later realized that if you give in to fear, fear will haunt you for the rest of your life...until you finally stand up to it and confront it head on. "Get ahead of that thang!"

Affirmation:

What do you fear? You have to get ahead of that very thing that is holding you back. You were destined for greatness!!! You were built FORD TOUGH! Like the Bible tells us in Philippians 2:14:

"I can do all things through Christ which strengthens me." If you don't believe it, no one else will.

I'm sure you have noticed how you can get a song stuck in your head. It's easy for the mind to remember words that have been set to a melody or that have rhythm. There are affirmation CD's or YouTube videos available that are great for listening to in the car, especially if you are a commuter. Also written positive affirmations are one of the most popular positive thinking exercises. Some people write them out and place them on the refrigerator, mirrors. This can help commit them to memory until they become second nature in your self-talk. Give it a try and remember to speak POSITIVITY over your life every morning—make it a daily routine.

_____

_____

_____

_____

_____

_____

_____

_____

_____

Stay away from
negative people.
They have a
problem for
every solution.

Day
eighteen

REFLECTIVE THOUGHT OF THE DAY:
Don't allow the madness
around you to create madness
in you. Hold fast. Don't allow
nonsense to distract you from
your purpose.

Soulfood: ♡

Sometimes, we unknowingly give toxic
individuals influence over our thoughts,
behaviors, and feelings. It's important to
recognize when these negative individuals
intrude in your life in an unwelcome
manner.

Affirmation:
*The less your respond to negative
people, the more peaceful your life
will become.*

Guard your time. Don't allow negative people to steal your time and energy. Choose your attitude. Spending time with negative people can be the fastest way to ruin a good mood. And lastly, refocus your thoughts. Pay attention to how your thoughts change when you're faced with negative people. Identify the positive people in your life. Decide that you're not going to allow negative people to determine how you think, feel, and behave. Take back your power and focus your time and energy on becoming your best self.

_____

_____

_____

_____

_____

_____

_____

_____

_____

_____

_____

I fall, I rise, I make mistakes, I live, I learn, I've been hurt, but I'm alive. I'm human, I'm not perfect, but I'm alive.

Day
nineteen

REFLECTIVE THOUGHT OF THE DAY:

Everyone makes mistakes. Just don't keep repeating the same ones. Learn the lesson. Stop surrounding yourself with people who won't tell you the truth. The lies aren't helping you heal.

Soulfood:

Many of us keep making the same mistakes over and over again, and somehow we think that one day we're going to miraculously reach that holy grail of life... happiness. The key is to look at these perceived "mistakes" with compassion, and instead of beating yourself up for making the same mistakes over and over, learn to use them to your advantage.

Affirmation:
I have to learn to forgive myself for not being perfect.

Use this time to identify the mistake. Write it down. Figure out what making that mistake over and over is doing for you. Instead of beating yourself up for picking up a bad habit, focus on replacing it with something positive.

_____

_____

_____

_____

_____

_____

_____

_____

_____

_____

_____

_____

_____

_____

_____

_____

I always feel like I can do anything. That's the main thing people are controlled by: thoughts and perceptions of yourself... If you're taught you can't do anything, you won't do anything.

—Kanye West

Day twenty

REFLECTIVE THOUGHT OF THE DAY:
If you believe in such a big God, why are your dreams so small? Your Father is the King: exercise your Faith and go after your destiny!!!

Soulfood:
♡

You are fearfully and wonderfully made.
God thought of you before you were
even created in your mother's womb. He
has plans for you, to prosper you, to give
you hope. He's given you all you need
for doing what He has planned. And He
promises to bring his dreams and purposes
for you to fulfillment. God can do anything
far more than you could ever imagine in
your wildest dreams! He does it not by
pushing us around but by working within
us, his Spirit deeply and gently within us.
This scripture comes to mind:

*"But as it is written, things which eye
saw not, and ear heard not, and
which entered not into the heart
of man, whatsoever things God
prepared for them that love him"*
(1 Corinthians 2:9).

Affirmation:
*I can do ALL things through Christ
which strengthen me.*

Dedicate some time this week to dream in depth.
List the main areas of your life. Example: Relationship with God, other relationships, marriage and
family (current or future), finances, career, etc.
Under each heading, write your expectations for
that area. Now, prayerfully go back through the
list. Ask the Holy Spirit to reveal His perspective
and promises. Remember, God has taken the limits
off your life. It's time for you to do the same!

_____

_____

_____

_____

_____

_____

_____

_____

_____

I don't focus on what I'm up against. I focus on my goals and I try to ignore the rest.

—Venus Williams

Day
twenty-one

REFLECTIVE THOUGHT OF THE DAY:

Your victory is in YOUR vision. You are not limited by what it looks like right now. You cannot see what has yet to manifest.

Soulfood:

I've had some great victories in my life. God has set me free from many things. Being free from bondage is absolutely amazing, and it's something God wants all of us to experience. Don't live your life without the thrill of growing and changing, or you'll miss out on the good things God can do through you. You have to go through to get through..but oh the sweet victory on when you make it over...my GOD!!!

Affirmation:
It's time to start pursuing your goal. Don't settle and lose your edge. We weren't created to be mediocre. We were designed to be exceptional!

Answer these questions to clarify your God vision:

Is your God vision too small? If your vision doesn't terrify you, it's too small. God has already placed the gifts inside of you. All you need to do is find your passion. Remember, you must develop tunnel vision when going after your dream. You must be dedicated to your vision, study on it, educate yourself, eat it, sleep it, drink it, dedicate all your energy to mastering it. You got this!

_____

_____

_____

_____

_____

_____

_____

_____

_____

_____

_____

_____

_____

98

Omega

God is using your current
season to prepare you for
your due season. Your current
season may seem long, and
hard, but remember it is a
season of preparation.
God has a specific season
that He has set aside to
bring to fruition His plan and
purpose for your life.

About the author

Niya Brown Matthews is a Life Coach, Best Selling Author, Motivational Speaker, Radio Host of her own show Soulfood Sessions with Niya at Hot Noize Radio, 2 time Breast Cancer Survivor, Ambassador for Ford Warriors in Pink, and 17 year Real Estate Professional as well as Mother of a daughter who attends Georgia Southern University. She writes inspiring self help books to empower others to overcome their life obstacles and challenges in order to become successful in Life, Love & Career. She attended East Carolina University and is married to retired Super Bowl Champion Eric Matthews of the GreenBay Packers. They are very active in the Atlanta community running their non profit Eric Matthews Matthews Foundation helping low income families and at risk youth. Niya Matthews has been featured in numerous national media EBONY, Black Enterprise, Black America Web, Rolling Out, Mommy Noire & Wendy Williams, ESPN, and Essence Main Stage (twice) as well as featured in Today's Purpose Woman Magazine to name a few. She is founder of Two Fabulous for Cancer, a Charity Organization helping breast cancer patients fight the fight as well as the founder of Soulfood Sessions with Niya a Women Empowerment Organization created to uplift, and empower women globally. Her books are sold nationally at Barnes & Noble, Amazon and her website soulfoodsessionswithniya.com.d to shift the atmosphere if you're not willing to move your feet. Greatness is available to you, but you have to be open to receive it.

Connect with ♡Niya

www.soulfoodsessionswithniya.com

Social Media Handles

IG: @niyabrownmatthews
@soulfoodsessionswithniya

FB: @niyabmatthews
@niyabrownmatthews
@soulfoodsessionswithniya

Twitter: @NiyaBMatthews